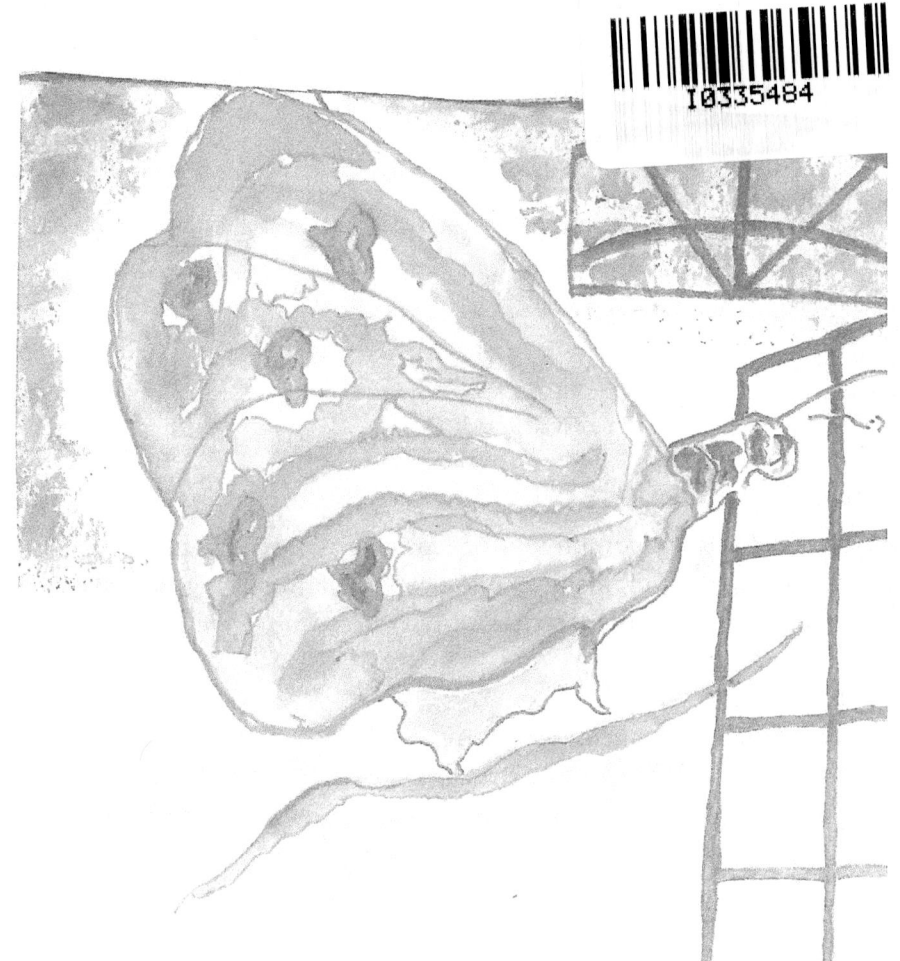

The Infinity Image
Patricia Earl

The Infinity Image
Written and illustrated by © Patricia Earl, 2019
© Cover illustration, Patricia Earl, 2019
www.patriciamearl.com

ISBN: 978-0-9941975-5-9 (paperback)

Lilly Pilly
PUBLISHING

No part of this publication may be reproduced or transmitted by any means (electronic, mechanical, photocopying or recording) without written permission from Patricia Earl: *patriciamearl@gmail.com*

All rights reserved.
Cataloguing-in-Publication data available
at the National Library of Australia

*For Robert Garstang.
For Olive Smith.
For David Smith.*

CONTENTS

The Infinity Image 1
Infinity 2
Rain 3
Cicada Time 4
Desire 5
Blue Remembered Hills 7
Sky Goddess 12
Wild Night 13
Seadrift 14
Seawitch 15
A Perfect Balance 16
A Mirror Image 17
Summer Love 20
Passion 21
A Cold Light 22
Infatuation 23
The Lost Eternal Light 24
See You Later, Cinderella 25
Landscapes of the Mind 28
Love 29
Sky Father 30
Jealous Time 31
The Sleep of Exiles 33
The Eternal Night 37
Last Words 38
Lost in Space 39
The Ancient Flame 40
Tears in the Sky 41
Connection 42

Penny for the Guys	43
Understanding	46
A Hurricane Blast	47
Flower Power	48
A Short Summer	49
Surf and Turf	51
Strawberry Child	54
The Colour of Truth	55
Dreamtime	56
A Season of Discovery	57
An Indian Summer	58
Outfoxing Lyndsay	59
Borders	62
Seas of the Soul	63
Summer Time	64
The Mission	65
A Winter Feast	66
River Time	67
Taniwha	69
A Winter of Earth's Desire	72
Moon Madness	73
Full Moon	74
Rainbow Goddess	75
All that Glitters	77
Tiger Lilies	81
Dream Tapestries	82
An Ulster Plantation Katikati	83
Skies More Tropical	84
Over the Bar	85
Skull & Crossbones	87
Hamilton's Frog	91
King of the Beasts	93

Devil's Advocate .95
Active Service 97
Evening Sun of Memory 100
A Backup Performance 101
360 Degrees 103
Afternoon Time 106
Castles in the Air 107
Lullaby 108

About Patricia Earl 113

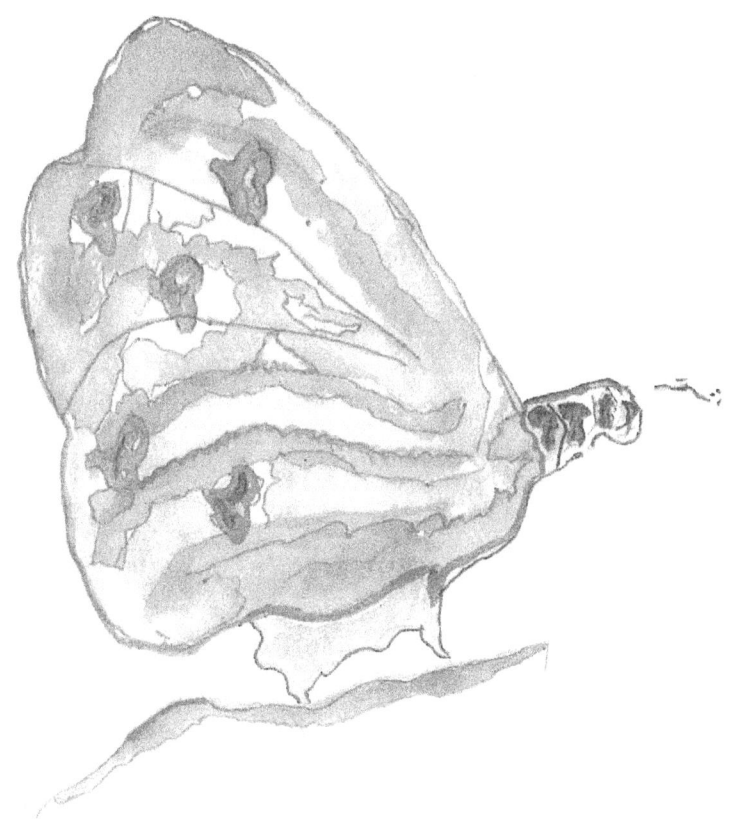

The Infinity Image
Patricia Earl

THE INFINITY IMAGE

First there was the ocean
and with courage the land,
when the sea returned
what it couldn't understand.

So what was left to reflect
was a silver sea of sand.
At high tide a dreamscape
of another mirrored land.

In the sea's froth and still
we can still walk on dreams,
as the spirit dances over the
mirrored edge of infinity.

INFINITY

Time after time
is like a snake
chasing its own tail
as the ancient tales go.
Memory stays in
the moment and
the future is the time
the gods will play.
So time is a circle
circling a circle
in an infinite way.

RAIN

A pattern of rain on glass.
A sidewinding half diamond
marking an ancient flame
with the scent of the aggressor.
Your ways are much older I fear.
And outside the translucent drops
linger like heavy pears
in a wire dance of faith
as our words balloon into
differences with the wind
and the understanding of rain.

CICADA TIME

Summer blossoms like a lover
high on cicada time.
A summery distraction from the
winged beat of time.

But like a thief in the night,
Winter on a midnight note
struck the final chime.
It began to rain.

On the idle hills of summer
I come and go like summer rain.
Tuned into your restless energy
on the horizon of our minds.

DESIRE

Once there was the dream
of rocks edging water
and the sea was the only thing.
A shared thing like laughter.

But in the testing way of things
when we reach for some desire
the mermaid nets are cast aside
for the maturity of fire.

And beauty in its inner form
is sometimes not enough
to show the cruelly testing fire
poised beneath the passionate slip.

And now the hardest thing of all
is to recall a siren song.
To clearly see the ledge and
hear the splash of the watery past.

And know the pain of mermaid foot
in the closing of desire.
To mourn now the iridescent scales
and the giving up of form for fire.

BLUE REMEMBERED HILLS

Hills blue with distance touching the sky. Land falling very quickly to the waiting sea. An Ulster Plantation four generations on. Settlers sailing to a land they had never seen. They must have thought luck was on their side.

This was morepork country. Morepork wings stopping at every shadow or every station if it's the morepork train. The main railway line ran through the original family farm.

But if the train trip from country to town and then on to the city took forever, the unsealed main road wasn't much better. Gorges cut off the region dramatically so there was a closed in feeling. The range of hills like warriors waiting. A watchful presence under a hawked sky.

And morepork problems were the reason for Harvey's visit to his father's farm that afternoon. That haunting, 'more-pork,' demanding sound stretching like wings over the gully and up to their house. For owls do fly.

After city life Erin felt small in this remote landscape even though she was tall for her age. The raw bones of the cleared land softened only by a few pines. Bush breathed over farm boundaries and when night fell whispered ancestral secrets that were frightening. It sounded like the bush was talking to her. Trying to tell her something.

So that afternoon Erin was watching the unsealed side road for any sign of dust rising which would indicate a car coming. She had the front gate open for her brother, Harvey, to drive right up to the house without stopping.

He stepped out of the car, with a paper under his arm, and smiled as he tipped his hat at his sister. As usual, when going out, he was smartly dressed in jacket, white shirt, tie and good trousers. Appearance and reputation, postwar years, were important in a small community where everyone knew everyone from way back.

Harvey frowned as he glimpsed the Massey Ferguson tractor defying gravity in a red flip before it got tread again and laboriously made its way up the steep hill. His father, Jim, was taking risks again to get the work done. His youngest son, David, was working nearby. It looked like he'd have to take refreshments up to them later for their break.

The small house, perched on the edge of a steep hill, was cramped but Dorrie had made it cheerful enough. She'd worked hard that morning baking scones and getting pikelets ready. She was more practical than fussy and didn't mind if the cups didn't match. Dorrie was a townie and used to more going on around her than she now got on the isolated farm. She'd been a nurse in a city hospital.

She was looking forward to Harvey's visit. He hadn't taken sides in the disputes over divorces and remarriage. He'd kept coming up to the city to see his father and new baby sister. His visits encouraged Jim to consider returning home to the place he felt he belonged and had grown up in. But their return home hadn't been very welcoming.

As the big teapot brewed they talked about the Friday Night

pictures that everyone went to after late night shopping. Shops were closed weekends so supplies were essential.

Harvey was nice looking in a brooding sort of way until his face softened into a smile. He was naturally outgoing and liked to talk to people. Something his introverted father couldn't do.

And Harvey, as head of the family, was running the old farm on the flats in a very efficient way. His herd of pedigree cows was producing very good results. It was his closeness to his sister that had led to Jim phoning the night before to ask Harvey to come up to the farm and talk to his sister. No one could read a book, relax, talk or listen to the wireless while Erin was moreporking up such a fuss.

Harvey reached over for the weekly he'd brought with him. He opened it at a page with a picture of a baby morepork grinning at the camera as it held a cigarette it had grabbed in its beak. The morepork was showing off like a fluffy toy that had come to life. Erin laughed and asked for the picture for her scrapbook.

"Do you know what bird this is?" Harvey asked her.

Erin shook her head.

"There was a poem I liked at school. 'The moping owl does complain to the moon'. Isn't that what your morepork does. Or is he just on his own party line thinking he's important. Owls do cry but not when they're hunting. Then he's a silent shadow looking for mice."

Erin laughed at the thought of the morepork operating his own phone line to talk about himself. They shared their phone line with neighbours. She knew not every call was for them. The afternoon had gone well.

Dorrie reached over to collect the bright pink cover of the weekly to add to her collection already in the wash-house. She loved bright colours and wanted to dye her white bedspread pink. As she put the mason jar of hot tea and scones in a basket she noticed again just how alike the brother and sister were. They were happy in each other's company. And both had that Irish colouring. Dark brown hair and fair skin. The twenty year age gap really didn't seem to matter.

Harvey shivered suddenly as though someone was walking over his grave. He'd remembered that old saying that if one hears three, 'moreporks', in a row then there will be a death in the family. He shrugged off the thought as negative.

Harvey helped Erin over the fence and they made their way down the cattle tracks, skirting the small stream where the house water supply came from. Just above, in a shallow pool, three pigs were wallowing in the slippery mud. Harvey had his good clothes on so they just laughed and walked on. Erin told Harvey how the cat had jumped up on the bench and whiskered through the scones. Her mother had had to trim them.

Time passes, but with courage, fear can't come flying back. Erin saw a morepork asleep in a tree and sat down to watch it. Startled, the morepork opened those wide starey eyes but it was half blind in the strong afternoon light. Erin heard soft, 'boo-boos,' lullaby sounds as though the owl was trying to make itself feel more comfortable. Then it launched into a sharp, shrill, shriek, cross at being disturbed.

And sometimes things can be too much. Too much to deal with. Like that morning her mother had rushed out of the bedroom to call the doctor and in her haste forgotten to take Erin with her. She was standing at the bedside of what was now the sickroom. The shocking pink bedspread seemed so out of place. It seemed to stare her in the face as the horror happened. Something, suddenly, had come flying through the window. There was no time for goodbyes.

And the trigger for all of this had been the morepork train whistling through the old family farm on the flats when a strong coastal wind was blowing. The driver frantically blowing his horn but he couldn't stop the train in time. The cows were on the railway tracks and the wild wind was blowing. They were grazing there after someone, carelessly, had left a gate open.

Erin looked up at the morepork. It muttered a little and shuffled its feet before falling back into a deep sleep. She wished she could share this morepork moment with someone but when she turned around there was only the clear blue sky.

SKY GODDESS

Once there was the dream
of rocks edging water.
A sky puddle mirror
for a high goddess.
So the sun made mud pies
that the moon at full power
pulled into the spiky
eyelashes of a rock pool.
Sky lashed the eye closed
and rippled like a skin
before opening to the sun.
A mirror image so the sky
could see herself starry-eyed
or blowing cloud bubbles.

WILD NIGHT

Wild night of my desire.
Let there be no brake to fire.
Flame upon flame's smiling surrender
to take away my soul.

So hold the flame's fiery thought.
Burn at the stake's knowing pain.
Yield to the desired night's
wildest flames and love again.

And see the power of surrender
to bring back moon's lucid light.
Once again chance winged flight
for some desire of fire and ice.

SEADRIFT

The attachment was the clamp of seaweed feet
while the green branches threw their hair
in that maelstrom of currents around the rock.

And the tide was much fiercer then
than the sluggish roots now show.
Rock upon rock and long green hair.

Mouths fastened fiercely for their share.
And as the fronds were swept from there
the rock face seemed to cry.

SEAWITCH

The seawitch coils in voiceless dreams,
bloated breast and slimy tail,
surrounded by those other streams
that swim in the reflection
of her strange and grotesque eye.

To whisper to that breast of shell
the seaweed shifts of love.
How weightless the loss and grief.
The siren lyrics in a form.

Feelings that float like foam
until lifted from the sea.

A PERFECT BALANCE

If I could describe his face.
The horizon of his eyes.
The thought that there's another place.
The meeting place of earth and sky.

But on that converging plane
that measures our design
a perfect balance is brought
to find that true defining line.

And in that troubled reaching out
for something to define
at first it seemed that there was
mostly blue defining sky.

But later with a final truth
and the sense beyond all time
it seems that really after all
there is more of earth than sky.

A MIRROR IMAGE

The river of sand was fascinating with that mirror image. A silver lining left after a wave that broke up into many images. A surface shimmer measuring the distance between sea and sky, trapping images of people and seagulls into fractured pieces from another world. A broken looking glass kind of world.

The sharp edge of the sea a petticoat froth that ebbed leaving empty spaces to dream beyond reality. The infinity image Paul had warned me about.

"You don't put a second mirror where it can reflect the same line of sight. Most people would find it unsettling," he told me.

And Paul seemed to know what he was talking about. He'd hung my antique oil paintings, art gallery style, at eye level and carefully worked round my collections of china and lace cloths more carefully than expected. Only once putting his hammer down on an antique cloth.

He was an interesting handyman to have around. Slight of figure with an air of weariness and importantly some expertise in his field of work. But it seemed to me that there was a faded air of disappointment as though things had gone wrong in the past. His grey hair was close cropped but there was a feeling that I wasn't seeing something that was possibly hidden deep down.

It was as though his features retreated into an inner distance where he really did care but didn't want anyone to know this space. A landscape of the mind.

"I've become very cynical over the past few years," he told me flatly.

I saw him as a romantic worn down by life as though something deeply personal was locked away and the key hard to find. My Pandora curiosity was coming into play.

So next time we met I stared directly at him and I was surprised when he didn't avoid that gaze, as though, he too, was curious and wanted to know more about me. For the first time I saw his soft green eyes and the softer side of him. A camera image that flicked my mind back to thoughts of my father, who, too, had lived for work. That Puritan Work Ethic. And Paul had the same need to keep busy.

On his day off from his regular job Paul would often be available to work at my place and I looked forward to seeing him on those Tuesdays. But sometimes he didn't turn up or rang with excuses. Those islands of the mind I'd come to depend on, those safe places, now shut down. Dragons from the past arched their backs and hissed. Mentally everything was going out the front door. A front door that was already splintered.

"I'm sorry, luv," Paul apologised, touching my shoulder gently, next time we met. "We'll get there in the end."

His smile was accepting and his manner very warm. I asked what was wrong. He told me there had been health scares and urgent visits to the doctor. High blood pressure among other things. Then one Tuesday he ended up in hospital and rang me from there.

"Just in for observation," he said. "Hopefully I'll see you

tomorrow."

He was warned about stress. Told to take it easy. That he wasn't so young anymore. Not the sort of advice Paul would be prepared to listen to. He ran his own ship.

Next morning Paul finished off the varnishing of my new front door and then walked over to the tubs to wipe his fingers. But he picked up an embroidered cloth that was around for decoration instead of the rag I'd left out for him to use.

"What's the matter?" he asked, when I laughed. I pointed to the cloth in his hands which was now very crumpled and stained with varnish.

"That will wash out," he muttered. He looked a bit embarrassed.

But it really didn't matter because this was just the sort of thing my father would do when he was busy and pushed for time. Just an absentminded moment when he previously had always seemed so perfect. Paul had always seemed so in control but here was another layer to understand. A deeper level I'd have liked to know more about and a memory back in time.

After weeks of rain the sun was out again and things more hopeful.

SUMMER LOVE

Summer - late summer on the heath
and apart we think of love,
but it seems such an in-between time
when flowers have a purple heart.

So, I hope you will understand
with summer spreading through the trees,
wildflowers have a season but
love is a once - flung thing.

PASSION

Once I stood within your court.
The caught web of attraction.
The web of a beating heart like
a roughly sketched passionflower,
purple veined to calculate
the outspan of a closing circle.
How the beaked hummingbird hovers,
coloured tail of shot brilliance.
A sharp-eyed whirling dervish.
Blurred assassin of love.

A COLD LIGHT

You're the light of my attraction.
The sea touching the sky.
Reaching the edge of stars sometimes.
A dream living out the lie.

And your eyes the new frontier.
A clever mask of chrome and glass.
A mirror to a madness and
a sadness in that reflection.

Love is truth's cold child.

INFATUATION

The sound of his voice
is music filtering through the senses.
A rippling murmuring stream.
A wave that moves forever.

And in the senselessness of things
in the summer's clasp and fall
in the reaping of experience
lies the pampered fall.

THE LOST ETERNAL LIGHT

There's a place where water-lilies
stir and weave against the light
to cast shameless seeking glances
at a rival seeking light.
And against the bright confrontation,
the scattering of the light,
mirrored there on the water
is the lost eternal night.
The other side of leaf and petal
and the shading of the form.
In the colliding of the senses
the thoughts that hold a stubborn heart.

SEE YOU LATER, CINDERELLA

Things aren't always as they seem at the time. My husband offered to buy me new shoes as my birthday present. Smart, black, court shoes.

"See you later, Cinderella," the assistant called out, laughing, as we left the shop. I had tried on quite a few. But it was hardly a Cinderella moment when the prince rode off on his white horse shortly after. He had other palaces and places that needed him.

"See you later, Cinderella," was all he said.

And it's strange how those fairy tales stick in the wrong places. We remember the prince looking for Cinderella and the happy ever after ending of the fairy tale. What we forget is the misery that presents itself earlier on and has to be overcome. There's the empty castles and dark lonely woods. And the poisoned apple spell cast by the wicked stepmother. And Beauty herself had to kiss the Beast to turn him into his princely self.

But sadly I'm the silly Cinderella type who isn't so strong. The one who is always looking for her prince. The one waiting for her fairy godmother to wave her magic wand. But other people didn't see me as such a weak character.

"Too much hair all over the place," Norman laughed as we sat in the club. "I think I'll call you Gypsy from now on. You're always wandering about like a child of the stars."

This wasn't very flattering but it had a truth about it and I knew Norman was just trying to cheer me up. He and my husband had never got on. They seemed to resent each other. Not that Norman could be accused of vanity in any way. He was more beast than prince, being a large, untidy sort of person with uncombed, unruly hair. But there was a calm, healing energy behind the biting wit. His kind blue eyes always looked amused when he saw me as though he knew me better than I knew myself. He also realised how upset I was about my husband leaving. His jokes were his way of lifting my spirits out of the dark woods I'd been wandering through.

"Have you heard from your ex lately?" he asked, looking at me intently.

I told him I'd had a letter from my husband asking if I'd like to join him in England.

"I think this comes under the abused woman syndrome," Norman replied. "How much more do you want to put up with."

We seemed closer after that but I knew Norman was married. I still looked forward to seeing him though.

"I'm waiting for another heart operation," he informed me one afternoon. "I've put it off because of family problems but it needs to be done. I had rheumatic fever as a child which has infected some of it."

"Hope it's not fatal," I replied.

We were sitting outside on the smoking deck and for a moment the bush seemed to stop breathing and listen in as Norman exploded into a sudden rage.

Everybody looked into the distance, embarrassed at his outburst to me.

"Look at them," Norman laughed. "They think I meant it."

And that's when I saw another side of him. The lighthearted part.

"I think I should be more honest with you, Gypsy," he said quietly, leaning towards me so the others couldn't hear. "I'm not happy at home and would have gone years ago but for family."

It was then I realised Norman was trapped in a bad spell that he couldn't break out of. He smiled at me in that special way and rushed off. The next day when he met me the scruffy untidy look was gone. He'd spruced himself up, combed his hair and put on smart clothes. He'd also called into the clinic to arrange an appointment for the heart operation that was so urgently needed.

And in the beauty of the moment he was the prince I'd been looking for. But there are other fairy tales with very different characters waiting for the expected happy ending. And I wasn't the practical Beauty type who might have been able to prevent what happened next due to over-excitement. The Beast was now the Prince but he had the wrong sort of heart for a happy Cinderella ending. It was the wrong fairy tale with mixed up characters. The clock struck twelve and the rats were running from another unhappy ending.

On the idle hills of summer love lingers like a gypsy lover.

LANDSCAPES OF THE MIND

Imagine the belief
that you could map
the atlas of the mind
to find the compass
to what lies beneath
what's called reason.
And if you could mine
the lining and timing
to see what creates
those sea creatures
which rise from the
sea green ocean depths
that you are finding.
The slow rolling Theta
waves rising to creative
thoughts that climb
so artlessly into mind.

LOVE

Love in the beginning
gives passion a chance
but love returning
shifts the rain from
the mistakes of the past.
But is this the same love
the second time around?
Is it in love or pure love
that is taking the chance.

SKY FATHER

Sky Father is your passing
I mourn the brighter light.
Narcissus of the night.

Without sight I scan the skies
for a trace of the former glory
as clouds hide your veiled face.

Perhaps you found the perfect love
and smile now from the heights
and gaze into those pools of light.

JEALOUS TIME

Against the mourning years
and the buds waiting to open
the white roses blow and
watch with those corner eyes.
Possessive like a lover,
enemy in your own land,
like time you cannot age.
And still I dream of eternal things
like the return of moon and tide.

THE SLEEP OF EXILES

This holiday, a brief break from the mainland, wasn't working out because there wasn't enough to do. And the rural charm reminded her of the farm she had grown up on back home. The farm she'd grown out of by the time she'd turned fourteen and needed more excitement.

Penny was finding out she didn't like islands because she felt exposed in some way. Their farm had been like an island in its isolation which shut out the rest of the world and things around them. There hadn't been anyone her age to talk to or play with. Isolation brought feelings of panic. Islands made her feel exposed like that afternoon she had been dancing out in the front garden in her petticoat after her bath. She was watching for any cars going past on that lonely side road. Her mother was angry with her even though the petticoat was like a dress with lots of tiny buttons so she was covered up top to toe. There were things about the adult world she had yet to know.

But on this small island she felt again that feeling of panic. Of being too much on her own. Left to her own devices with nothing to do. Where once the land had always been there like a green sea now she was surrounded by a cold, grey sea that was oceans away from the Pacific greenness she was used to.

Fortunately this holiday was nearly over but the disturbing memories kept flooding back. She remembered kicking the old ghost cabbages in their market garden. Cabbages turned white with age. Shrunken, because they hadn't been picked in time. Her parents were always so busy making a new start late in life.

And the hard work meant that very soon they could buy a farm which was what her father really wanted. One right up in the hills overlooked by the ranges. There was just a hint of sea in the distance to remind her there were other things than hard work and daily grind. Things of the spirit. Things like the bush ghosts whispering round the farm boundaries when it was getting dark. The rain whispering on the roof as she tried to read a book.

Books had been her lifeline though her mother would smack her if she caught her reading. She wasn't just being harsh about jobs to be done. She thought it unnatural for a child to like reading so much when there was fresh air outside and plenty of other things to do.

So Penny was interested that a famous writer had once lived on Guernsey and that, he, too, had found it confining and limiting what he wanted to do. To him this was the sleep of exiles. He'd been banished from Paris for expressing his views so openly on the current regime there. And Paris had been his lifeline because there was so much to do. Quiet, rural charm wasn't what he was looking for. It felt like imprisonment.

So it was then that he turned to spiritualism as an escape from the monotony of his existence. Regular séances were held for family and friends to listen to messages conveyed by table tapping ghosts like the famous Lady in White who had supposedly haunted this island for hundreds of years. The spirits were about.

But unfortunately the spirits weren't well behaved and they didn't always wait for invitations, calling late at night, knocking on the bedroom walls when the writer was trying to sleep. Singing could be heard somewhere in the house late at night. Papers were picked up by an unseen hand and scattered. Negative energies and emotions had been aroused and wouldn't go away.

Excitement turned to unease as the family felt the strain. His wife left for Brussels but he continued to write each morning. His muse, like a fading flower, bringing inspiration and comfort. He found the universal line in, 'every bird that flies holds a thread of the infinity in its claw.' This writer always looked for the beauty and the essence of things.

This is proved by his actions. Snakes and toads infested his garden without any action being taken to remove them. Two ducks his cook had brought home for Sunday lunch were quickly released outside. No flowers were to be picked and brought into the house.

Penny found these details very interesting and felt she knew the man behind the writer. She liked his alternative universe and the feeling of being inside the story now. And this story wasn't as tragic or miserable as the themes of the writer's novels. This brought out the grasshopper tendencies in her mind as she flitted from one detail to another and in the end choose the wrong spot that he'd made his favourite spot in Guernsey.

He had found an old seaport appealing. It had an interesting background having once been part of the French mainland. There was even a ruined castle to add to the magic and best of all this place wasn't that far from town. Although this move never happened Penny wanted to see this spot for herself. It was that castles in the air kind of giddy feeling that she couldn't resist checking out for herself.

If Penny was searching for castles in the air she found them in this isolated spot. A spot the writer had never been to because it was too far out and he was a man who loved the company of family and friends.

The correct place was actually only a few miles from town. A place she could have approached safely, walking along the sand. Without being certain she was in the right place Penny walked over the grass to the stark cliff edge. The cliffs were chalky and chalk can be slippery.

After the farm years Penny was used to hilly high places and knew how to turn her foot carefully into the side of a hill like cattle did. And after all this was a place of imagination she wanted to wander through. Looking for Victor Hugo she fell down the cliff.

THE ETERNAL NIGHT

Night steals the light
as dreams stream across the bar
to the soul's eternal night.
Like a low lingering tide
there's only dark shadows.
A reflection of the light.
And now the sun isn't rising
and there's only morning
but in mourning such a loss
love floats on a wave
that will last forever.

LAST WORDS

Why do I miss you so much?
Why is life now so empty?
You were the perfect one.
I wonder if you knew that.
Things we take for granted
are sometimes not explained.

Why do I want you so much?
I wish things hadn't changed.
Perhaps you were insecure
and told a few lies.
But in the end nothing matters
if I could once again have the
chance to look into your
skyblue eyes of feeling.

LOST IN SPACE

Like a wave crashing
on a distant shore
we were running against
the rising moon tide.
The spirit dances
but we flew too close
to the midnight sun.
The wind swept us away
and now you're out there
in another place.
In space like a lost star.

THE ANCIENT FLAME

Life it seems is fleeting.
Nothing it seems is for keeping.
Time passes but nothing lasts
and evening takes the light.
In the very vastness of the
before, now and ever after
sea of understanding I know
you were my pulse and life.
If there could be a return
from that big beyond
how I'd be there
to meet you.
Things we know now
we didn't know then.
Love's in the understanding
of this ancient flame.
If only we could have
the chance again
but love in its own way
is still a wave that
moves forever and forever.
The lover wave to the
waiting shore.

TEARS IN THE SKY

Tears in the sky
like diamonds.
Light stars of
another dimension.
Footlights of
another show
that's more than
the stars know.
Tears in the sky and
diamonds forever.

CONNECTION

In the house of beautiful thing,
in the midst of my collections,
in the dust of memory past,
the family albums and photos,
letters and cards we've exchanged,
you remain my best connection.

PENNY FOR THE GUYS

We remember with pleasure past Guy Fawkes nights in this country where this was an outdoor get together for lots of fireworks and excitement.

'Remember remember
the fifth of November.
Gunpowder, treason and plot.'

Bonfire night was like being on another planet. The fiery sparks and dark having their own conspiracy. Night has that special secrecy of whispers and things unseen going on in the dark.

And the celebrations lent a warmth that held people together. A fuse so to speak. About a month beforehand a man would go into the bush to find just the right tree with a Y fork to stack the other branches into a tepee style. Paper and cardboard were saved up to help get the bonfire going on that night.

And our guy would be a sack, stuffed full, with a garish face painted on him. He'd be put pride of place, on the stack. And it would be great fun with the kids all over the place. But that's years ago now. Just a memory now that fire and safety regulations have put an end to all that.

So we were feeling a little bit fed up this bonfire night. The only big firework display we were likely to see would be a fiery eruption from one of the many volcanoes our city is built on. This island, volcanic to its molten core, might rise up, just for us, in a fiery fury. Byron was getting a bit fed up.

"And you'd better watch it," he shouts at Rangitoto sitting quietly in the distance. "They'll be after you too."

The volcanic did not reply but the empty loo rolls Byron had put on a string round his neck rattled in sympathy. He knew he had the wrong period. Stuart, not Elizabethan, but he went with the idea anyway.

But we should have brought our fireworks earlier because all the shop had left was girlie sparklers. But we couldn't turn our noses up at sparklers because then we'd have nothing to set off some sparks. Unfortunately Guy Fawkes had been born some four hundred or so years too early to help us out when we needed his expert advice.

So this was the question we asked ourselves. What would Guy Fawkes have done in the blow up scenario with only 432 sparklers to work with? A mini rebellion but one we thought worth pursuing.

After some thought we put the sparklers into small bundles and then bigger bundles until we had a sheaf of sparklers not wheat. We wanted the best max flash.

I pulled the centre sparkler up to act as a fuse that would set the others off. We lit this fuse and suddenly there was a fountain of sharp, hot sparks. Who would have thought little girl stuff could get so dangerous and out of control. And still the devilish device hissed in a whirling, dervish, mad dance.

The hot, hot sparks burnt through our clothes and onto our skin. The mercury was coming through our boots as we frantically tried to stamp out the running sparks. Our backyard was electric. The air white with fury. The tips of the grass were alight and the string clothesline and pegs blazing merrily. Byron's jacket was alight and the window in the garden shed gave an ominous creak. I grabbed the hose.

We could hear the siren going off and realised just how far out of hand our joke had got. We'd a lot of clearing up to do before the landlord called again.

We were absolutely filthy but the discarded sparkler stems mirrored delicately the pinks and greens of the thistledown skyrockets just above us. And of course we still thought we had the best display and had shown a bloke's inventiveness with very limited resources. And in the process we'd upset the next door dog who was whining at our fence and scratching to get in.

All in all it had been a very good bloke's night in.

UNDERSTANDING

In the land of understanding
the wind doesn't blow and
rain doesn't whisper on the roof
thoughts causing hurt and pain.
There's no sharp staccato drops
falling as sleet or snow as
though something's wrong.
In the land of understanding
love isn't looking for perfection.

A HURRICANE BLAST

I know the way of hurricanes
and that deep trough of despair.
That locked inward feeling spinning
in a mad dervish dance.
And I have that inner feeling
not to temper tempering forces
by force meeting force when
you simply answer back in defense.
So the answer is to take cover
from that anger and aggression
and understand the hurt feelings.
That the hurricane's ultimate blast
is about the distance of things
that lie in the unresolved past.

FLOWER POWER

A red flame smoulders
and works the red magic
that makes the blood flow
in hibiscus flower power.
So veined in glory and
petalled as hearts show
and open to the sun's
suggestion about spending
power and birds and bees.
Showing off the moment
so new life can grow
from tomorrow's seeds.

A SHORT SUMMER

Summer sharpens the senses
like a snake moving
through the grass
as the spirit dances
through a short summer
which wasn't even a summer
except for the sensibility
of it all.

SURF AND TURF

Sea. Land. And that same old battle. No wonder this place was called Spirits Bay. And the Tasman sea was in a blue mood with wind and swell gathering in strength. Not a good day for an important fishing competition with a big stake of $1500. That was the prize money offered for the biggest snapper caught up north this day.

And Muzza's group were ready for the challenge. Muzza had arranged this trip and forked out for any extras needed. Chance and Shout were just part of the town, Friday nighters, and along for the ride. Muzza liked being the central clown of that crowd.

And this was usually just the right spot for snapper to hang about. An oval flash of silver and gold showing they were around. A sudden shimmer of silvery pink colouration with a flash of iridescent blue lighting up a wave. Big, 'Moocher', opportunistic feeders, dropping in for the pipi and mussels found here.

Chance found the wind was against him and the strong swell threatened to knock him off his feet as he tried to cast his line out. The sea was in a wild mood as though trying to put him off but Chance enjoyed a challenge and things going against him. He had the necessary muscle and strength to fight the sea on his terms if he had to. Then it happened. The flash. That bulgy head. The biggest snapper he had ever seen. Chance fought to keep the line steady as the snapper's head thumped in those last minute tail shaking runs but just when he thought the fish was his it got away.

Chance took the disappointment in his stride. He had that winning way with the world in that he never let things get him down. He was a chancer by name and nature. He'd disappear when it was his turn to buy a round only to reappear a little later when it was a mate's turn to buy the drinks.

And Chance had a scary grin that waved trouble away. A Cheshire Cat sort of grin that lingered just a little too long for comfort. Surface charm waving over everything.

"You should have seen the beauty," he boasted. "Those jaws could have broken my finger just trying to take the hook out."

It was Muzza who gave up early. He handed his rod to Shout who'd been rounding up on the other competitors like a stray dog. Annoying them with unwanted advice and silly remarks. Shout was more than eager to have a go and soon his luck was in. He soon had a snapper that was just over the legal limit. He left the snapper on the rod as the rules required for the later judging. Not that there was much of a chance in the scheme of things.

It was Shout's job to get the barbeque going and put the steaks on as he enjoyed a Dominion Bitter beer. Muzza, as usual, was centre stage telling jokes and laughing all the time. As a builder he could afford to be generous and he often had work going. Chance was a reliable worker but Shout, in Muzza's opinion, was virtually unemployable as he lacked the necessary strength and muscle.

Shout was unpopular with his bitter comments about mates even after they had shouted him a beer. He had the bristly aggression of a stray dog handed out bits and pieces of scraps. But he was making a good job of the steaks. Muzza fancied a bit of snapper as well.

When Chance got a word in he landed a few dirty jokes with his usual relish. He'd got them all thrown out of a smart pub for his remarks to a staff member. For once Chance couldn't understand it. They'd spent heaps on food and drinks. That made him angry.

The day, all told, had sort of slept in. The sun coming out at the last possible minute. The judge turned up to see what they had caught. He glanced briefly at the empty hook then turned to go.

"Who got the prize then?" Muzza asked.

"No snapper caught up north all day," the judge replied.

The news took a while to sink in. Muzza was looking a little sheepish. For once he was quiet but Chance took it in his stride as he doubled up, laughing all the way down to his boots.

But for Shout this disappointment was the final nail in his coffin. He had the right nickname and he carried it to the limit about the unfairness of it all. He'd been the one who'd caught the only snapper there that day and the money would have been his.

He shouted all the way back to the city but it was too late. Nothing would put the prize snapper back on the hook. They'd eaten the only snapper caught up north that day.

STRAWBERRY CHILD

Rachel Rachel
running wild.
Rachel Rachel
strawberry child.
The freedom of innocence.
Like a tiny bird
reaching for the light.

THE COLOUR OF TRUTH

Mary's a problem in the park.
Trailing around with a jeering laugh.
The old truths come tumbling out
like nasturiums over rocks.

She's sharper than a magpie's eye,
sheer madness on a branch,
but sometimes when she can't fly
Mary seems frightened of the sky.

DREAMTIME

In the land of impossible dreams
dreams can last forever
skylifted to a sky plantation
on another planet
that's way beyond Mars.
Where the only connection
is with the imaged stars.

A SEASON OF DISCOVERY

Love can be a bitter season.
Bitter in part or whole.
A season of discovery
that shows another part
of what's eternal.
Anger tears at the soul.
Nature written with
a careless hand.
Doubt and grief
have much to sow.

AN INDIAN SUMMER

The falling tears of Autumn
are now the Winter of my soul
as the spirit dances through
an idyllic Summer for a day
of summer pleasures
in an Indian Summer.
A quick embrace
and a slow forgetting.

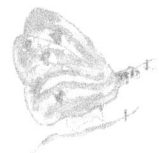

OUTFOXING LYNDSAY

The Harlequin Pub was rightly named for the comedy played out there. We'd meet up on a Friday night after work. The same group at the same table. Friends of a sort. More like acquaintances really.

And they say never judge a book by its cover or in this case a man by his jacket. A tweed jacket worn with white shirt and jeans. Quite the country look. Lyndsay had been minding a farm for some mates while the owners were away.

My first thought was a foxy one. A Mr Todd one from the Beatrice Potter tale. He'd worn a jacket that probably was a very gentlemanly green. This was a Tommy Brock badger jacket, tweedy and short cut. Opposing characters and different jackets.

I asked Lyndsay whether at heart he was more fox than badger as I commented on his jacket.

"Badger," he answered quickly. "I'm not a fox. I'm not sly or cunning."

So there was no mental divide opposing the physical. No pure thoughts battling with lust and putting a gentlemanly face on things.

And Lyndsay had the same square build, black spiky hair and white skin that was the badger colouring. He also had that same lascivious grin. At times Lyndsay could be disruptive, outrageous and seek to shock.

"There's something of the beast in a man," he told me with his son of Satan grin. "Casual sex is best."

But casual can be too casual at times. Like the time Lyndsay's car had caught fire in a passionate moment because of the pulled down seat in his Vauxhall car being too close to the battery. He'd had to remove the seat and beat out the flames.

But under his tweedy air Lyndsay could be two different people. Either friendly or distant. So we only knew what the moment showed. His blue English eyes at times looked very distant. Foxy eyes showing no emotion. Mr Tod in the story had been a pretend gentleman with the right manners. Tommy Brock, on the other hand, grinned all the time but slept with one eye open. Like a blocked drainpipe once cleared he could be ready to go. Lyndsay had picked the badger character as his own but the fox, deep down in the depths of his soul, was just as bad.

But it took an invitation to the Museum to find the real Lyndsay. His main interest it seemed was being a volunteer guide at the neo Classical style Museum and he invited us to be his guests the next Saturday afternoon for a private showing.

"Do you like my jacket?" Lyndsay asked me eagerly. "What do you think about my jacket?" His jacket was dark and more formal than usual with a slight fleck which was in character. This was worn over a white shirt and dark trousers. He looked very smart as he escorted us around the Museum and eagerly answered our questions. He knew his stuff.

A little later I slipped away from our party to commune with Raj, the elephant exhibit, on display. It was then that I became part of Lyndsay's commentary.

"She's got a short attention span," he shouted out to anyone who was listening. "She's got a thing about elephants. I think it's the trunk."

And much later we were back in the middle sanctum entrance looking up into the inner pyramid of light high above. This was a very moving past and present moment when everything seemed to come together.

At around four o'clock we were ready to head back to the Harlequin for drinks after a very fulfilling afternoon we'd all enjoyed greatly.

Lyndsay paused for a moment to look back at the Museum. It seemed to be floating in its own classical moment over the volcanic hill as though it had always been there.

"This place gives me a voice," Lyndsay commented quietly, his eyes looking into an inner distance. "That's why I come here. It makes me feel more peaceful."

BORDERS

Time is always on my mind.
Doomed like Penelope to endure
tropic dreams and kapok cloud.
Border lands of hope and despair.

Hope like a crazy patterned quilt
crossed with the memory of love.
And love of passionate commitment
spread over to comfort and last.

And setting in like bad weather -
despair - another crazed seducer
in motley jester's brilliant garb -
is painting the tropics a ghastly red.

Grey light's splendid duellists
but unable to finally kill
the love that brought us here.
Borders and love returning.

SEAS OF THE SOUL

Those oceans of feeling
in the seas of the heart
have that undercurrent
that keeps us apart.
In the seaweed shifts
and rocky ocean floor
are the sandy attachments
that reach the seashore.
Those seas of the soul
and passions of the heart
subconsciously seeking out
what keeps us apart.

SUMMER TIME

Moments of the heart
of our summer love
as summer glides
as a rising moon tide.
And the days linger
like another dimension.
Softly falls the light
from the moons of the sun.
Inscripting that part
of the ancient flame.

THE MISSION

The soundless exit of a doubt.
Will that be the final fear
in the night riding of a mission?
Unbridled doubt without a rider.
A death without honour in the field.
The epitaph for a soldier.
The dark rider who always came home
or a kind of death from within.

A WINTER FEAST

Memory has its own hunger
as a goldfinch is back
looking for winter seeds
and summer is remembered
in a late flowering hibiscus
after Autumn's sleep of decay.
Winter's the holding pattern
as buds form on the trees
for Spring's wild desire
of green fire.

RIVER TIME

At high tide the river rides
carried by the sea.
Boats rock and bells ring
like islands of ecstasy.

At low tide or on the turn
the river drifts and dreams
in mermaid streams until
the waves wash her hair.

TANIWHA

The club was spacious in the wrong sort of way. Roomy with more of a canteen feel than a restaurant. There was a dark bar area for cheap drinks but no comfortable easy chairs to sit in and relax.

Even the ocean breeze seemed to be after something. On the make for something that might be there. Ocean views and open shutters letting in a lot of hot air. No wonder the club was known around the district as the Nazi Club because of the bullying General Manager and his insistence on his own rules being kept and adhered to. His focus was usually money. So the club was badly managed by the one at the top who had all the say.

There wasn't a nice atmosphere but one of the staff had obviously had better training in better places with higher standards of excellence. He was paper-thin and worked with tremendous body energy in a nice way. He had that dark European charm and flirty French ways that amused members and took some of the bad feelings out of the scenario. It was his place and he set the scene.

But Jacques didn't take his popularity lightly. He insisted on standards such as the proper setting of tables and in the posher upstairs bar he commented on the tablecloths being placed upside down carelessly.

"Can't they see the hills and the valleys," he muttered, referring to the ironed pleats. "And you never show the table top when changing a cloth," he added. "That is just not done."

But he was fighting a losing battle in the way the club was run. Newspapers for members use were binned in the morning, music was played too loudly for conversation and bar staff were told to serve drunk customers even though this was a breach of liquor licensing laws.

But in a short time we found a connection and became close friends. We muttered about the club but looked forward to meeting up again. Jacques was always attentive with extra slices of lemon in the glass of water he'd bring me and even fetching a glass of wine so I didn't have to wait at the bar when the club was busy.

Jacques moved with a fluid grace like a current knowing where it was going. There was an inner force that drove him to work even harder as though he was making up for something only he knew about. An inner compulsion to work harder than necessary. He swam with the currents he knew so those dark swirling depths weren't on show. A man very much in the moment in that French approachable way.

But everyone has a boundary that shouldn't be crossed. When Jacques hit the dark side he was like a river that had burst its banks after too much rain had fallen. Then the usually loving side of him was gone as the current turned on itself. A breaking point until the problem on his terms was solved.

Not that that even happened in this club with its lack of standards but by the next day Jacques would have got over it and be back to his usual friendly self. And when he got the chance he'd stop by or sit down at my table.

"You're my only break," he'd say with a warm smile. "You make my day."

He was told not to fraternize with members but he ignored this ruling. It was a very healing connection for both of us with the warmth he generated so easily despite any personal problems he might have.

But being club related one day this might end. In the meantime there was that river spirit meeting the wide blue ocean view of not caring about anything as long as the money kept rolling in. That ocean hot air of the club's atmosphere.

But in the bowing and greeting of the French connection the river spirit was winning. River spirits can be good or bad but this taniwha spirit was on the right side.

A WINTER OF EARTH'S DESIRE

Winter summers in
a red hibiscus
and a goldfinch is
back on seed memory.
Winter the holding
wing and starting fuse
as buds show green desire.

MOON MADNESS

I know the way of madness
like a witch before the moon.
That scorpian kind of twist
to that irresistible attraction.
And the tidal pull of dreams
in the final movement of the turn
that will twist the face of fish
drawn to that surface too soon.
And in the moonshine of our dreams
and those arrows to the heart
is a wild profanity of toadstools
breathing out their poison as
puffballs push through the grass
in similar ecstasy hoping to
steal that glassy sadness.
The soul born out of suffering
in the hunting of the moon.

FULL MOON

Alien moon
your light reflection
opens up the sky
to a lunar madness
that seems to mirror
our own experience.

A clown in the moon
looking at us with
that staring sadness.
But on a clearer night
you're a soul seeker
seeking higher skies.

RAINBOW GODDESS

After sunset softly falls
watercolour pastels paint
the horizons of the sky.
And after a rainy day
what's painted in streaming
colour is the dispersion
of the sun's rays in
falling drops of light.
Then Isis with her bow
replenishes the rain clouds
with water she's lifted
from the sea for that
natural kind of healing
between sea and sky.

ALL THAT GLITTERS

Auckland's a city built on thirty-five extinct volcanoes. Mountains have their own way of sorting out problems. Usually by a violent explosion of built up steam from things that have been going on for some time. And it was moments like this that I was about to find out on this particular Christmas Day sort of evening.

I had an invitation from a friend to join her for a dinner at a Chinese restaurant in Mount Eden. An area so named because of its refined, paradise regained sort of air. The eruption had taken place a long time ago and now streets wound round the sheltered side of the mountain and the wooden villas whispered their Victorian lacey secrets.

One could think nothing bad would happen in such a genteel kind of place but I was soon to find out this wasn't necessarily true. This Christmas Day had a funny kind of feeling as though something was waiting to happen. A waiting, brooding, closed in feeling like the mountain itself was thinking out loud. Something was in the air like high tide when there's no wind, just a little turbulence in the air. A feeling that anything might happen.

After quite a long bus ride across the city I had drinks with Laura and her husband at their Eden villa and later after the meal, dessert back there. They were both very welcoming. But something seemed to be bothering Laura, as she was a million miles away from her usual, vivacious self.

Although Laura was over eighty time hadn't found her yet. She was tall, slim and always very fashionably dressed in boutique clothes that she chose carefully. And she was fun to be with. Outgoing and friendly. Always laughing but for some reason not this evening. This was her more serious side.

As Laura was driving me to the bus stop she started to tell me what had happened in Mount Eden just a few streets back. It had been playing on her mind.

"I don't usually tell people this," she said quietly, "but two of my grandchildren are adopted. My son took them in when he heard about their plight. Their father had killed their mother."

I didn't know what to say. It was a sudden shock to have this brought up so suddenly. There weren't many details about the reason for the murder. The woman had left Sydney and moved to this district in Auckland but her husband had tracked her down. The ripped skin on her fingers and arms showed how hard she'd fought for her life.

So it wasn't only mountains that blow up violently leaving that blown out scarred crater. The boiling hot mud from the deepest level of hate for one who had once been loved.

When the mother had opened the front door unsuspectingly he'd stood there with eyes of hate glittering with distorted emotion. A terrifying image like the warrior gods at the Museum with their glittering paua shell eyes. Hate makes someone kill the person they once loved. Hate rises like an angry weapon and destroys. In this particular case the weapon found was a hunting knife.

At the city bus stop Laura parked her car and joined me. She was back to being her usual cheerful self.

"You don't think I'd leave you on your own on a day like this do you," she laughed.

And the road was deserted of people and traffic. Most people were at home or with family on such a traditional day. Then a man came into view from the city end. He was around fortyish and rather rough looking. He walked past us but then turned sharply and stood behind me. It was a tense moment as we wondered what he wanted.

"I've got $80 in my pocket," he growled. I froze and couldn't answer.

"We're not interested in your money," Laura informed him very firmly. She knew how to stand her ground.

He walked away and we watched until he was out of sight. I looked back at the mountain still dominating the landscape from this distance with its imposing shape. Benign now but once very destructive.

On the ride back I couldn't stop thinking about the attack and the seven heavens of hell which had landed that night. When the police arrived the children were crying and clinging to their mother's body.

Laura's son, John, heard about the children being in and out of foster homes, unable to settle as they relived the trauma over and over again. Their sense of security was split. Soft toys and cuddle rugs brought no comfort. It hadn't been easy for this family adopting the children and bringing them up as their own. In the end it was tough love that was needed. John paid for any therapy the brother and sister needed himself.

I usually saw Laura at the local club on a Saturday night and on one occasion her grandson, James, was with them. He was a teenager at the higher education stage, thinking of job prospects but Laura thought him a bit of a lost soul. Despite all the family efforts he was still dependent on them and somewhat ill at ease with others of his own age.

The story of our Christmas offer on the road came up and the grandfather was laughing.

"$80 offered for the two of you," Don laughed. "I hope you two don't think you can make a living at it."

James laughed at the story of the unexpected encounter. He said he was hungry and looking forward to his dinner.

He was talking quietly to his grandfather about something. Laura looked at him anxiously but since he seemed more relaxed now she flicked back to her usual self. Taking over the table as she laughed and talked in her animated way.

More glamour than glitter, she just liked being out for the evening and enjoying herself. James looked at her and smiled, amused at the attention she was getting. She was the centre of attention in a nice family way. Family that had gone a long way on a difficult road to make up for those moments when a mountain of hate had been exploding.

TIGER LILIES

Tiger lilies spring divine
in the gardens of my mind.
Jungle souls of strumpet brides.
A promise of another kind.
To last forever in the spite
of ancient eyes breathing night.
So wait until those amber fists
fade into forgetfulness
as the soft poison casts its spell.

DREAM TAPESTRIES

In the castle of all time
turrets and towers reign sublime.
The lofty structures
of higher thought
woven as dreams into
the rich tapestries
adorning the castle walls.
And floating in the castle moat
are the circling thoughts
of empty air denied entry
into the castle of all time
which bubbles under a perfect sky.

AN ULSTER PLANTATION - KATIKATI

A range of hills the colour of distance
close like a fist on an Ulster landing
like the Red Hand battle for land
fought so many years ago.
A settlement landlocked, seablocked,
now highjacked by the supple-jack spirit
of bushsickness preventing the progress
of a dream promised new land.
Unsummered bush needle fingers
twist and knit under a hawked sky

SKIES MORE TROPICAL

In officer blue
the pukeko struts
across his swamp
on full parade.
Like Caliban he's
more earth than sky
with that same dismal cry.
But there's a hint
of skies more tropical
in that proud flick
of his white tail.

OVER THE BAR

Please play me another ballad
because life seems out of tune.
There's that old-fashioned feeling
of a metronome beating to
the time of a romantic heart.
There's a soul to all feeling
in that irresistible attraction
of the note going over the bar.
The romantic islands of love
played in ballad fashion.

SKULL & CROSSBONES

Everyone loves a pirate because they have that daring audacity to do what they please and take what they can get. So the pirate entertainer at the local surf club on Friday nights was a very welcome figure greeting diners waiting for a table and then showing them their place.

And there was that ocean setting anyway and the horizon. Anything could happen and the only witness might be a parrot. This was a tourist spot with an ocean front, a wide river mouth and lots of winding canals. Water everywhere for those, 'Sail Ho' shouts and the first glimpse of a skull and crossbones flag. Bounty on the way if they kept up the pressure. Fascinating unless your boat was on the agenda or a galleon was in the harbour.

And Captain Ratty would of course be overfamiliar with his chat in an amusing way.

"I saw you watching me with your beady eye," he shouted. "Don't you think I'm working hard enough?"

His glinty eyepiece was fixed on me. Perched on his nose was a red bead to give that grogblossom, rumsoaked piratical look. Rum, the right drink to give pirates the courage for their plundering and raiding. Storming of the boat and the climbing on-board.

"Can I be your Polly?" I asked him.

"Of course you can, my Polly. Hop onto my shoulders. Arr. Shiver my timbers, won't I look after you."

I liked him standing over me with that high piratical energy. It was like a wind coming off the sea but under the banter I sensed a connection as though for once I'd got in first and caught him off guard. In a quieter moment he told me a little about himself.

"I'm happiest when I'm on show," Grant told me. "I feel much more at home with myself when I'm not myself."

I'd always been interested in the theatre and understood the attraction of being someone else for a short while. Someone different. Another character in luvvie terms like me pretending to be the pirate's parrot. The real person coming out from behind the mask.

Grant was of slight build but Captain Ratty was big and burly. A lot had to go into each character to make it convincing enough for the diners facing long waits for their tables.

Captain Ratty made a point of stopping by when he got the chance.

"Hullo, Polly. My little treasure," he might shout. The black feathers on his hat dancing. The silver and gold chains around his neck swinging. He was mad, bad and dangerous and his wicked smile said it all. And when night is nigh pirate's needs need meeting so they say.

"You were great last night, Polly," Ratty shouted. "I left your money on the fridge."

He turned with a flourish to see if everyone was listening. He liked to throw in this sort of cheeky line.

"I can't give you any change," I replied in Polly fashion. "I need that for crackers."

With a wink Captain Ratty was back on the pirate trail. And

that trail must have been a thunder and lightning kind of life. On the run all the time with an eye out for trouble. Frequenting houses of ill-repute where rum-laced folly was going on.

As the pirate entertainer Captain Ratty had such a delicious energy he could get away with anything.

"Would you like to pick the barnacles off my bottom, Polly?" he asked. "Careening they call it."

He winked at me. By now I had the feathered energy and licence to say anything I wanted to.

"Well, I've got a sharp enough beak for it'" I replied.

It was all a lot of fun and we all got on so well on the surface of things. One afternoon outside the club a man approached me, smiling as he held out his hand to greet me. I didn't recognise Grant at first. He looked so different in ordinary gear.

One night another pirate walked in for a drink. The physical energy needed was on show but there was no thought behind the character playing. This pirate was loud, crude and happiest with a drink in his hand and mates around him. He thought he was top mast but he couldn't have got up the rigging very easily without help if he had to and time is of the essence for that sort of skulduggery.

But Grant had other characters to play to keep up the entertainment level. And perhaps I was too involved with the show myself. Far too many squawks and feathers that could be ruffled. Not enough finesse but then that's what parrots are like. Top of the birds in parrot thinking.

One Friday night, Grant entered in costume as Manuel, the little, insecure waiter from the series. To flesh out this character he took tiny steps and kept looking down nervously. And perhaps I was feeling a little jaded or just plain sulky because I wasn't getting the attention I was used to.

"Where's my pirate?" I demanded as Manuel nervously shook

my hand.

"If you're in tomorrow, Polly, so will he be," Manuel quietly assured me.

But Manuel must have had some memory loss as the next character to show up at the club was Lily. She swanned into the bar area but didn't stop when she saw my pained expression.

On the way home the courtesy bus driver laughed when I told him how I'd been stood up by a pirate. He knew Grant well from sharing meal breaks with him in the staff room.

"He's just an old hippy," he explained. "Old in the sense of being stuck in a rut. He's polite to a point and doesn't say much but you have to watch what you say or he'll argue."

So yes I know most parrots live longer than their pirate owners who get beaten up and injured. Then they limp along and end up in books and pictures with one eye missing and a parrot on their shoulder. A more loyal parrot than I had been and not such a show off.

HAMILTON'S FROG

Please spare a thought for me.
I'm Hamilton's frog
now found only on a small bank
on a New Zealand island.
I'm a frog but I'm not green
and I don't croak or
have webbed feet.
With my toes I can push food
into my mouth very easily
and climb up trees.
I have a glandular ridge
behind my eyes which are large
so I can see in the dark
and the stars see me.
I'm a male frog who watches
and protects my tadpoles
wrapped up in slippery slime
to keep them safe and moist
until they hatch with already
developed eyes and legs
as they wriggle and swim
onto my back for safety.
A season of froglets

slipped into existence.
But I don't want to live
one hop from existence
or share the silence
of the dinosaurs who were
around when my frog type
was born so many
millions of years before.
So please protect me.
I go back to the edges of time.
I'm Hamilton's frog
on the edge of existence.

KING OF THE BEASTS

The giraffe has two little bumps
above his puzzled frown
on which to wear his golden crown.
So when he looked up or down
on stayed his glorious crown.
He was a kind and gentle king
so the animals felt at ease.
He lived on lots and lots of leaves
that he nibbled from
the tops of trees.
Summer thunders with a roar.
Is that lion five miles away
or just next door?
Night watches over the King
as he's fast asleep like
an orange breath of Heaven
but just before eleven,
like a thief in the night,
the lion lifts off the golden crown
and hides it under his mane.
Daylight broke like a bad spell.
The Giraffe King wore a puzzled frown.
Has anyone seen his golden crown?
Now fear like a dark mask

walks the African plains.
Who now is King of the Beasts?
Although the giraffe is suspicious
he knows to keep his distance
because the new king
has a ferocious roar
and rules with a heavy paw.
Out on the African plains
a giraffe is gently strolling and
a monkey's eyes are rolling.
But the giraffe still has that
rolling gait and royal regal
look of state and those
two little bumps for a crown
that he wears above
his very puzzled frown.

DEVIL'S ADVOCATE

Hell's full of empty promises
as you're only too aware
but grace is offered freely
so the promise is still there.
There's so much to be banked
if you take your mind off care.
Now to take care of this debt
how about shares in your assets
because all that glitters is gold
and just waiting to be sold.
No more empty green promises
from that garden of despair.
For the assets and dividends
on account are still there.
On offer is a different kind of
saving so let's turn loss into
profit and not be so openhanded
in showing that you care.
Heaven is an investment that we
as shareholders are aware
that it is there for the taking.

ACTIVE SERVICE

On this afternoon there was a remembrance service upstairs at the local surf club. Support for the Veterans who had served in Vietnam fifty-one years on from when it started. Originally it was an American Police Mission.

But what was being honoured today was the Australian side of the war in Vietnam. The Australian troops were trained in anti-guerilla warfare. Their operations relied on stealthy patrols by small units through jungle, rubber plantations, rice fields and villages. Enemy forces faced against main-force regulars who could ambush them at any time.

Thick vines growing through the rainforest made it difficult to spot a target from an aircraft so Agent Orange was sprayed down and the vegetation burnt three days later. Jungle warfare has its own problems and although the troops were well trained enemy forces were the ones with the tunnel systems and local knowledge. Things were never going to be easy and there was pollution of the water system.

The Surf Club seemed the right place to bunker down as another storm blew up the sky in an aggressive rage. Lightning flashes adding the strikes to the uprising as a witchdoctor kind of wind danced madly round the sandcastle hotel blocks in a mad frenzy.

Later that afternoon some of the men moved downstairs to the general bar for a few beers and rum chasers. I asked about the night patrols.

"Oh, it was all lit up," Bryan told me. "The jungle I mean. Phosphorescent from all that rotting material. We could see alright and in that situation your night vision improves anyway. And we had fireflies stuffed into jars which we kept round our necks so we kept up with the one in front for protection."

Gary had been on the airforce side and he considered Aussie planes to be the best at backing up assaults with strikes when there was action but on one occasion the Americans had got the co-ordinates wrong and hit the wrong target which was the Kiwis. Apparently the American planes had been too high up.

Bryan had liked the jungle because it gave him protection until Agent Orange came down like a grey mist killing everything.

Outside the storm rolled on and inside the club so did the humour.

The New Zealand side were mostly artillery I was told.

"We needed their backup. They called on us to get over quick to get them out of a troublespot and just about a week later we called on them to get us out of strife. We called them fat-arsed chickens and they called us hawks," Bryan explained.

By now the storm was easing off and taking the trouble with it. The talk turned to how unpopular this war had been back home. There had been protests and demonstrations. No support for those who had risked their lives. Gary told us he couldn't even go into a pub and buy a beer like his mates because he was underage.

"I was alright," Bryan laughed, "because I was twenty-one when I got back."

Bryan and Gary were strong survivors but others hadn't been able to cope well with combat-related stress and the horror they had been through. A gunner had been defending fifteen mates under attack when his machine gun jammed. He had to seek help in order to cope with what had occurred.

"My husband was in the Korean war," a wife told me. "He got frostbite there, and he was also in the Malay one. But it was Vietnam that did the damage."

EVENING SUN OF MEMORY

The evening sun of memory
records as a final flash
things we need to see
in a higher light.
Another day is over
and now just a memory
as twilight softly celebrates
that passing moment's grace.
Night falls in the dying
light of inner feeling.

A BACKUP PERFORMANCE

Green isn't the star performer
in the stage performance
as a backdrop cover for
colours to be serenely seen.
Green is the background colour
on the artist's palette
just waiting to be seen.
Nature written with
a careless hand
shaping chaos into
a perfect scheme.
Backgrounds are second nature
in the heart of things.

360 DEGREES

My life isn't a short story. I've lived too long for that to be true. I'm five foot two, eyes of blue and a bit of a lad. I'm a poet and know, it so here's a sample of my work.

> 'She sits in the corner,
> in an elegant recline.
> Diamond rings on her fingers,
> clasp a glass of wine.
> Tall, statuesque,
> perhaps an English Aristocrat
> she could be.
> She says she's forty-nine,
> and who I am to disagree.'

And one afternoon at our local club I remember telling my forty-niner friend my most embarrassing story which happened in New Zealand on a jet-boat trip. We had thought this part of the country a bit samey. Either green or scrubby but the falls we were visiting were stunning. Plenty of water coming over the face. The soft spray as ethereal and high as the mist on our Scottish hills.

We were swept under the overhanging branches and right up to the foot of the falls. Strapped in, wearing life-jackets, hands clutching the heated rails doing 360 degrees in the jetboat. We were warned about keeping our jaws clenched because of the G Force and centrifugal spins but it really hurt.

My face was screwed up like a torn melodian like I was in space. It seemed likely that my false teeth might fly out as a macabre offering to the Huka Falls. I could imagine that empty evil grin at an eel meandering past through the mud.

Anyway that didn't happen and although the day itself was rather dour we enjoyed the jetboat trip and falls very much. So much so we couldn't resist stopping the next day on our way home at the big waterslide adventure park. Since I had no togs with me I put on a pair of denim shorts.

For safety reasons we were timed and I was first down the slide only to stick like glue at the first bend. With no slip or give with the denim I could only sit there as the water piled up behind me. I had the most awful feeling that I might drown in my own bodyweight of water. I'd become my own waterfall.

It's like when you're spinning so fast in a centrifugal spin you stay exactly where you are and don't travel. And I was the pin. Feeling very trapped I looked up at the open bits in the slide so I wasn't completely shut in but I was stuck fast in a pipe with water building up and over me with nowhere to go.

Fortunately, my wife Minnie, came down the slide, crashing into me. My legs went up in the air and off I went only to stick fast again at the very next bend and so on in this undignified manner until we both splashed into the bottom pool.

We got up only to be knocked over by the next people coming down the slide. Staff rushed round with grappling hooks worried about our safety rather than our dignity. Very sheepishly we got out of the water and went back to our car. Too late we saw the warning notice about the importance of wearing proper swimming gear before attempting the slide.

Being Scottish naturally we're pretty canny with money but this time we quickly decided not to claim or use our remaining slides. It had been a right disaster and that was that.

But my best moment will be when I take the best spin of all as a bit of a lad and it's way in the future. This will be when I undertake my last journey of all and get someone to throw my ashes in the Clyde. That's way in the future of course but being such a careful person I've already planned it.

At Port Glasgow's mirren shore I'll travel with the tide to the Firth and on to Rothesay Bay to drift past the Cumbrae Isles and round the Arran Coast. Then to complete my 360 degree spin I'll return homeward through the Kyles to Port Glasgow, the place I love the most.

Such a spin would be a very fitting end to a life filled with travel. But well in the future of course.

AFTERNOON TIME

As the sun slides into
the seductive dream
of afternoon time
the moment is ripe
for the picking
as bees hover over
that ancient flame
of their desire for
a new beginning.
It's a green harvest
as the pulse of life
throbs on the promise
of the summer of all time.

CASTLES IN THE AIR

Somewhere there's a castle
and a magic stair.
A fantasy dancing on
a high wire of despair.
And desire's fire fires
such thoughts to the flame
so be careful
what you ask for
on that magic stair.
Dreams are empty castles
floating in the air.

LULLABY

Be careful what you wish for
as wishes can come true
like a magic carpet ride
after a visit to the zoo.

Safari plains look like fun.
The giraffe is gently strolling
but the rhino's kicking up a storm
and his eyes are rolling.

Animals are not at home
when walking up your path.
And can you walk a tiger
or put a hippo in your bath.

A dark forest isn't safe
with a wolf at your door.
So shine a torch brightly
until he holds up his paw.

Fishing is lots of fun
in your canoe made of bark.
Catching a sprat is fun
but what about a shark?

Can you put a hat on a bat?
Fit an elephant in a tent?
Share a dare with a polar bear
and a cake with a snake?

So be careful what you wish for
especially after dark.
Creatures come in all sizes
and they love to roam about.

Patricia Earl has published five children's books.
The Importance of Being Moki
Pipi Visits The Jungle Pet Shop
Moki's Crystal Palace
King of the Beasts (awarded 2016 RADF arts award)
The Peacock Palace Elephant

Background

BA English Literature & Philosophy Massey University
website: *www.patriciamearl.com*
2009 Second Prize Jack Diamond Essay Competition Waitakere City Council

Reviews

Goodlife Magazine 2017
Patricia Earl's series of children's books are beautifully illustrated with her bright handcrafted paintings. Fun books for the family.

Our People
Patricia's active imagination brings her characters to life.

www.ingramcontent.com/pod-product-compliance
Lightning Source LLC
Chambersburg PA
CBHW050436010526
44118CB00013B/1561